Darkest Night, Brightest Dawn: A Lent Reflection

Philip Yeung

Published by Yeung E Publishing, 2022.

Table of Contents

To all who feel the spirit is willing

but the flesh is weak

Darkest Night, Brightest Dawn

.

Dr. Philip Yeung

.

© 2022 by Joanie Yeung

.

.

Cover design by Joanie Yeung

Foreword

Thank you for picking up this Lent book!

For many Christians, Lent ushers in a process of deep introspection, repentance and renewal. It compels us to take a solemn look at the painful passages in the Bible that record Jesus' betrayal, his struggles in the Garden of Gethsemane, his unusual trial by Pontius Pilate, his agonizing time on the cross, as well as his death and burial.

The four Gospel authors highlight different details of each of these events, and their choices shed light on the true essence of the Good News. None of the Gospel authors presented our Saviour as a mighty superhero slaying the enemy, but instead we see a human being, one full of humanity, authority, understanding, forgiveness and obedience to the Father's will to the end, and this is where the Good News is found. In the Garden of Gethsemane, in the darkest time of his life, our Saviour embraced the most painful struggles, sorrows and suffering of humanity and showed us God's answer to all of them. Every detail from that fateful weekend reveals a deeper aspect of the relationship between God and us.

This book is the second product of the translation project my family has been engaged in as part of our hope to continue the legacies of my father, the late Pastor and Doctor Philip Yeung, by publishing and translating his talks (The first translation is *Jesus' Awkward Questions* published in 2021). This Lent series is based on a collection of seven sermons he preached at Emmanuel Chinese Church, Hong Kong, in Spring 2012. Each chapter examines the historical events that unfolded, starting from Jesus washing his disciples' feet up to Mary Magdalene encountering the risen Lord, and reflects on what Jesus accomplished for us when he said, "It is finished" on the cross. As both a medical doctor and a professor in biblical Greek, Philip Yeung liked to dissect the texts by looking at the Gospel authors' original word choices and expressions in the historical and cultural contexts of Jesus' world, while his focus was always on the Godhead incarnate.

The concept behind the cover design of this book is based on two references to blood and water in the Passion of Jesus: the first one was found in the Gospel according to Luke, a physician, where Jesus' sweat "became like great drops of blood falling down to the ground" (Luke 22:44) because he was in great sorrow; the second was found in John's account of Jesus' final moments on the cross when a Roman soldier thrust a spear through Jesus' side, and at once there came out blood and water (John 19:34), thus confirming he had truly died. Both instances testified to the magnitude of the emotional brokenness and the pain of the physical death Jesus went through.

This book aims to retain all the core messages, analyses and life applications in the original sermons. In translating the Chinese sermons for a Chinese audience from the spoken form into written form for English readers, some general discussions and examples used in the talks have been paraphrased for better readability, and details that are specific to the local contexts of Hong Kong have been omitted. The discussion questions at the end of each chapter were added by the editor to encourage study groups to engage with the contents and exchange ideas.

Our sincere hope is that this book will bring renewed strength to all those who feel weak in any form of struggles, an eternal light to those living in darkness, insightful discoveries to those studying the events of Good Friday and the resurrection, and the good news of salvation to those who are seeking Jesus. We pray this book will be helpful both to Christians who have been walking with the Lord as well as seekers of the Christian faith who are getting to know Jesus.

Joanie Yeung

Betrayed

.

(John 13: 1-30)

.

Have you ever been in a situation where you knew someone was going to betray you? What did you do? Indeed, Jesus has, and he knew exactly what was going to happen down to the smallest detail of his death that would follow. In John 13, we see Jesus spending the evening and sharing a festive meal with his closest friends, including the one who would betray him that very evening. How did Jesus choose to spend the evening with him?

We begin our Lent journey with the night of Jesus' betrayal. All four Gospels record details of the evening before Jesus' death, but while Matthew, Mark and Luke put the spotlight on the Last Supper, John has chosen to record something totally different: the story of Jesus washing his disciples' feet (John 13). It's not surprising because John often writes about details not found in the other three Gospels.

We're all familiar with the famous story of Jesus washing his disciples' feet. We love the warm fuzzy feeling we get as we try to picture Jesus' humble posture bending down at the disciples' feet. We are touched by Jesus' radical humility in choosing to do something only the lowliest servants would have to do at his time.

Yet, have you ever wondered: if washing feet is the focal point of the story, then why is there only one sentence in the entire chapter (John 13:5) depicting how Jesus did it? What happened in the rest of the story? What, then, is the author really trying to draw our attention to?

The real focal point of the story

The opening line of the passage reads,

> **Having loved his own who were in the world, he loved them to the end. (John 13:1)**

Here, loving 'to the end' is not referring to a specific time frame, but to the extent of the love. It means the love will extend to the absolute maximum level. For God, this would indeed be an extent way beyond human imagination and understanding. It meant there is no limit.

Let's read the story very carefully once again and see what we notice.

> It was just before the Passover Festival. Jesus knew that the hour had come for him to leave this world and go to the Father. Having loved his own who were in the world, he loved them to the end.

6

2 The evening meal was in progress, and the devil had already prompted Judas, the son of Simon Iscariot, to betray Jesus. **3** Jesus knew that the Father had put all things under his power, and that he had come from God and was returning to God; **4** so he got up from the meal, took off his outer clothing, and wrapped a towel around his waist. **5** After that, he poured water into a basin and began to wash his disciples' feet, drying them with the towel that was wrapped around him.

6 He came to Simon Peter, who said to him, "Lord, are you going to wash my feet?"

7 Jesus replied, "You do not realize now what I am doing, but later you will understand."

8 "No," said Peter, "you shall never wash my feet."

Jesus answered, "Unless I wash you, you have no part with me."

9 "Then, Lord," Simon Peter replied, "not just my feet but my hands and my head as well!"

10 Jesus answered, "Those who have had a bath need only to wash their feet; their whole body is clean. And you are clean, though not every one of you." **11** For he knew who was going to betray him, and that was why he said not every one was clean.

12 When he had finished washing their feet, he put on his clothes and returned to his place. "Do you understand what I have done for you?" he asked them. **13** "You call me 'Teacher' and 'Lord,' and rightly so, for that is what I am. **14** Now that I, your Lord and Teacher, have washed your feet, you also should wash one another's feet. **15** I have set you an example that you should do as I have done for you. **16** Very truly I tell you, no servant is greater than his master, nor is a messenger greater than the one who sent him. **17** Now that you know these things, you will be blessed if you do them.

18 "I am not referring to all of you; I know those I have chosen. But this is to fulfill this passage of Scripture: 'He who shared my bread has turned against me.'

19 "I am telling you now before it happens, so that when it does happen you will believe that I am who I am. **20** Very truly I tell you, whoever accepts anyone I send accepts me; and whoever accepts me accepts the one who sent me."

21 After he had said this, Jesus was troubled in spirit and testified, "Very truly I tell you, one of you is going to betray me."

22 His disciples stared at one another, at a loss to know which of them he meant. **23** One of them, the disciple whom Jesus loved, was reclining next to him. **24** Simon Peter motioned to this disciple and said, "Ask him which one he means."

25 Leaning back against Jesus, he asked him, "Lord, who is it?"

26 Jesus answered, "It is the one to whom I will give this piece of bread when I have dipped it in the dish." Then, dipping the piece of bread, he gave it to Judas, the son of Simon Iscariot. **27** As soon as Judas took the bread, Satan entered into him.

So Jesus told him, "What you are about to do, do quickly." **28** But no one at the meal understood why Jesus said this to him. **29** Since Judas had charge of the money, some thought Jesus was telling him to buy what was needed for the festival, or to give something to the poor. **30** As soon as Judas had taken the bread, he went out. And it was night.

If we are to observe closely the proportion of description to which John has assigned various characters and actions in the whole narrative, we might be shocked to find out that John 13 is as much about Judas as it is about Jesus. The chapter certainly puts more spotlight on the relationship between Judas and Jesus than the act of feet washing itself. Judas was mentioned again and again throughout the passage, and we can see the tension escalating as Jesus gradually hinted more and more at his knowledge of what was in Judas' heart.

Jesus' act of washing his disciples' feet was radical and shocking, not only in his humble and intimate way of showing love, but also in the fact that he *also* washed the feet of Judas, the betrayer.

Washing Judas' feet

In other words, John not only emphasized Jesus washed the feet of Peter, who had no clue what was going on, but those of Judas as well, who was just about to betray his Lord. As Jesus knew full well that Judas was preparing to leave soon to go to conspire with the people who would torture and kill him, he could have easily delayed the washing and waited until Judas had left the room. Then he could have skipped washing Judas' feet.

However, what we see here is that Judas was included intentionally, not by chance. Jesus chose to include the feet that would go and deliver him to his painful death. Jesus made sure to wash Judas' feet just before Judas left to betray him. We know this was a deliberate act because later, in verse 18, he quoted Scripture to explicitly reveal that this was what he was doing: "He who shared my bread has turned against me" (verse 18). In the original Greek text, 'turned against me' was literally 'lifted his heel at me' (i.e., kicked me).

Jesus' love was not an ignorant one, but a radically unconditional one, one that comes with full knowledge and insight into the darkest parts of our hearts. This is the love that loves *to the end*. Love is an abstract concept, but in Jesus, we see tangible, visible and concrete embodiment of what love really means.

We can hardly imagine the emotions and thoughts Jesus was experiencing while washing Judas' feet. And if Jesus took the initiative to wash Judas' feet on the night of the betrayal, how much more is Jesus willing to wash your feet so that you can be clean? There is absolutely no one in this world whose feet Jesus would not be willing to wash.

An unconditional love that has no end

Notice Jesus did not wait for Peter and the other disciples, who were totally oblivious to what was happening, to first understand Jesus' salvation before washing their feet. He did not wait for Judas to repent or give up his devious plans. Jesus acted with love first. Whenever we face our own sin, shame and darkness, there is one thing in life we should always remember: Jesus is ready to wash your feet right now and make you clean. He is not waiting for you to understand everything. He is not waiting for you to be 'good enough' for him. He is good enough for you. His towel is already wrapped around his waist, and he is already bending down to wash your feet, because he has chosen to love you *to the end*.

You may wonder, who are "they" in verse one that says "he loved them to the end"? The passage also highlights the idea of belonging. Jesus loves all those who are "his own". This is how Jesus looks at us. We belong to him. We are his own. This is why in verse 8 when Peter was initially reluctant to allow Jesus to wash his feet, Jesus solemnly pointed out the horrifying consequences of not being washed by Jesus: he would have no part in Jesus. Peter understood the seriousness of this statement and immediately adjusted his preference. Good choice, Peter.

We belong to Jesus. When he washes our feet, he is not just serving some acquaintances, he is cleansing his people, his own flock.

And Judas was also Jesus' own! What does this mean to us when Jesus commanded us to wash each other's feet? We are not only to serve our friends with love and humility, which is not too difficult to do. We are to wash Judas' feet as well, the feet of those who would inflict the worst wounds on us, just as Jesus did. We are to love our betrayers until the end.

A love that comes with full authority and knowledge

Please note Jesus' love was not a pessimistic, fatalistic kind of surrender. Jesus was not putting up his arms in the air and saying, "Fine! You win! I give up." Jesus' stance comes with 100% authority and victory. First, the story highlights how Jesus fully knew what was happening and what would happen (13:10-11, 21, 26). So, technically, Jesus was not really betrayed, because he was in complete control of what was to happen to him.

Imagine if you knew someone would betray you, and you already knew exactly the details of the plot, do you think this person could still carry out his plan successfully?

Imagine there is a mole inside an agency. The mole thinks he is secretly penetrating the organization to carry out a detrimental deal to bring down the boss. Yet the boss already knows who the mole is and all his plans and schemes. The boss is only allowing him to exist in the agency to further the boss' own purpose which the mole is not aware of. Now the mole is no longer a threat, but just a pawn piece that the boss is using for his master plan.

This was what Jesus' relationship with Judas was like; yet Jesus *still* included him when washing the disciples' feet and loved him to the end. How did Jesus reveal his insights and love at the same time? Notice how in the story Jesus gradually revealed his knowledge of Judas' plan bit by bit. First, he said that not everyone was clean (verse 10). Later, he quoted Scripture, "He who shared my bread has turned (or lifted up his heel) against me" (verse 18, quoting Psalm 41:9). Afterwards, he was troubled in spirit and hinted more explicitly, "Very truly I tell you, one of you is going to betray me" (verse 21).

The intricate art of exposing a betrayer

This statement Jesus made (verse 21) must have been so shocking that it made everyone at the table nervous. Eyes were open wide. Awkward silence. The disciples were confused and puzzled at what Jesus was trying to say because Jesus discreetly said all these things in a way that was only clear to Judas while keeping the others in the dark. Their confusion was also probably because betrayal was such a disgraceful act that they could not imagine that one of them would ever do such a thing.

In the final revealing, when the curious disciples had to ask Jesus who exactly he was talking about, Jesus chose a common dining table gesture to reveal who the betrayer would be (verse 26). In fact, in Jesus' time, a host dipping a piece of bread and passing it to a guest was a common act of hospitality, often done to a special guest of honour. The hint chosen by Jesus was so subtle that the disciples still did not get it. They simply thought Jesus was telling Judas to do some last-minute shopping for the feast or to give money to the poor, both of which were not unusual things to do just before the Passover.

Jesus was cleverly 'showing his cards' to Judas while still protecting Judas' honour and saving his face in front of his peers. There was no shaming, no public condemnation, no incrimination. While Jesus was passing the bread to Judas, he was giving a chance to Judas to come to his senses and change his mind before it was too late.

At the same time, Jesus was confronting Judas with two options he must choose from: either repent and turn around right now or go and carry out his planned scheme. There was still ample time for Judas to think this through while he walked out of the room with the money. If he changed his mind, he could still come back with some shopping, as if nothing had happened. No one else would know what was in his heart (except Jesus of course). Even until the end, Jesus was trying to save Judas by offering this perfect escape route for him, but history tells us that Judas did not take the offer. Ironically, the extent of Jesus' love is shown through Judas.

The price of loving to the end

John's account of the story contains a verb that is highlighted twice (observing the author's choice of verbs is always a helpful way of studying the Bible): the verb 'to do'. It first appears in Jesus' famous commandment to his disciples in verse 15, "I have set you an example that you should do as I have done for you." The second time was Jesus' command to Judas alone (verse 27), "What you are about to do, do quickly." The first 'do' is a practical action that is about humbly serving and loving even the unworthy. Yet what did Judas 'do' in response even after witnessing Jesus' love and having his feet washed by him? He chose to betray Jesus.

John also explicitly describes Jesus' emotions: he was troubled in spirit (verse 21). This is already the third time John describes Jesus as being sad and troubled between Chapters 11-13. The first time was when Lazarus died from his illness (Chapter 11); the second was when Jesus was faced with the imminent suffering and pain he had to endure as he accomplished God's plan. We may say both emotional instances were 'natural'; yet this time, Jesus was grieved by Judas' refusal to turn back even when given such an intimate encounter with Jesus' radical love and such a golden opportunity to repent. How pitiful, how tragic, and how painful!

During Lent, as we ponder the love that is shown through Jesus on the cross, do we see the extent of this love—the love that loves to the end even for Judas, and for you and me? Jesus has determined to love you to the end, to wash you and make you clean, and to provide you with a way to turn back. He never waits for any of us to accept him or to repent first. He first makes this decision to love to this unbelievable extent. It is up to us to be washed by Jesus, or to turn away.

Reflection and Response

1. How does the story demonstrate the extent of Jesus' love?
2. When Jesus commanded, "Go and do likewise", he wasn't only referring to washing our friends' feet but also our enemies'. How would you respond?
3. Do you truly believe God loves you 'to the end'?
4. How might this knowledge of God's love affect the way you view yourself, your relationship with other people, and your faith in God?

Weak

·

(Matthew 26:36-46)

·

36 Then Jesus went with his disciples to a place called Gethsemane, and he said to them, "Sit here while I go over there and pray." **37** He took Peter and the two sons of Zebedee along with him, and he began to be sorrowful and troubled. **38** Then he said to them, "My soul is overwhelmed with sorrow to the point of death. Stay here and keep watch with me."

39 Going a little farther, he fell with his face to the ground and prayed, "My Father, if it is possible, may this cup be taken from me. Yet not as I will, but as you will."

40 Then he returned to his disciples and found them sleeping. "Couldn't you men keep watch with me for one hour?" he asked Peter. **41** "Watch and pray so that you will not fall into temptation. The spirit is willing, but the flesh is weak."

42 He went away a second time and prayed, "My Father, if it is not possible for this cup to be taken away unless I drink it, may your will be done."

43 When he came back, he again found them sleeping, because their eyes were heavy. **44** So he left them and went away once more and prayed the third time, saying the same thing.

45 Then he returned to the disciples and said to them, "Are you still sleeping and resting? Look, the hour has come, and the Son of Man is delivered into the hands of sinners. **46** Rise! Let us go! Here comes my betrayer!"

When the flesh is weak

Jesus told his disciples who were struggling to even stay awake, "The spirit is willing, but the flesh is weak." Isn't this a highly accurate depiction of the human state? In this Lent season of reflection, we enter the Garden of Gethsemane and Jesus' most sorrowful and distressing moments. He knew very well the imminent suffering that was to come, and he asked his disciples, his closest friends, to stay awake and pray with him. But they all failed.

We might wonder why these men, all grown-ups, would fall asleep so easily at this critical moment. How dare they! Perhaps their insulin levels were running high after consuming all the carbohydrates from the Last Supper bread? Or they all had a few more drinks than they should in the Passover celebrations?

We have all been there. Every one of us has fallen asleep while praying or trying to pray. In fact, many of us might agree that praying is one of the most effective ways to fall asleep! Here, Matthew's account particularly points out that "their eyes were heavy". We all know exactly how that feels.

Luke, on the other hand, tells us that the actual reason why they were so sleepy was because they were "exhausted from sorrow" (Luke 22:45). Sadness numbs our body and drains our energy, lulling us into a drowsy, passive state. Have you ever been in this state? Sorrow prompts us to escape, and when our mind is too tired, too depressed, completely unable to face reality, the body chooses to escape by shutting down so that we stop processing the pain.

Please note that the Gospel authors never blame the disciples for being physically tired or rebuke them for falling asleep. There is absolutely nothing wrong with that. Sleep is part of God's creation! Jesus was not criticising but acknowledging that the flesh is weak. The problem was not physical weakness but the lack of spiritual vigilance and praying. They simply did not pray. What's wrong with not praying? Jesus' words tell us clearly the importance of prayer: "Watch and pray so that you will not fall into temptation" (verse 41).

The real problem is not being weak...

So, the point of praying here, according to Jesus, is about not falling into temptation. Whenever we don't pray, we become unprepared, blinded and confused, unable to process and respond appropriately to different situations in life. More than once, we see Jesus' closest disciples were still oblivious to what was happening. Despite Jesus' repeated explicit predictions of both his betrayal and death, the disciples were still insensible to what he meant. Again and again, they responded to the events that weekend totally inappropriately. First, they fell asleep. Then, Peter drew the sword and cut off the guard's ear, thinking that was the proper way to protect Jesus and themselves. After that, he denied his relationship with Jesus three times. Three times! In Jesus' most desperate moments, they all "(fell) into temptation" and fled.

What about Jesus himself? Did Jesus miraculously remove all the problems and overcome all the weaknesses like a superhero? No. Never in the Bible have we seen Jesus so distressed, weak and downcast. Spilling out his anguish, he said, "I am overwhelmed with sorrow to the point of death" (verse 38). Jesus was facing immense pain, and he was sad to the point of death. He longed for support, comfort and company, but found none.

We might wonder, why was Jesus so upset and hurt? Hadn't he been born for this very moment? Hadn't he come to earth just for this mission? We know the physical pain Jesus had to endure on the cross must certainly have been horrifying, but I believe that what was even more insufferable for him was the spiritual pain—Jesus would bear the sins of all people and be totally cut off from God because of this. This separation from God is the most horrible state in life. We humans are so used to being alienated from God that we become desensitised to this tragic state, unable to see its mammoth significance. But for Jesus, estrangement from God the Father was the most difficult pain to bear. Imagine all the sins in the world, including the most despicable sin of mankind, and all of God's wrath, would be on Jesus alone. The sorrow of Jesus was beyond words.

Shouldn't we be strong when we follow Jesus?

One message the passage gives us is this: the disciples and Jesus were both incredibly weak physically and mentally. Among Christian circles we often have this misconception that if we follow Jesus, life will be great and we will be strong. We believe that when we pray, we will be like Popeye gulping down the magic spinach and instantly becoming tough enough to fight evil. We think that the Christian life should be smooth, filled with peace, joy, hope, confidence, love, and immune to struggles, and everything should always be 'alright'. This would be a good testimony, wouldn't it? Actually, no. When Paul urges believers to "rejoice always" (1 Thessalonians 5:16), this "joy" does not refer to emotional happiness, but spiritual satisfaction. The Bible never expects us to be 'alright' all the time.

While both Jesus and the disciples were at their weakest points, the most significant difference between them was that Jesus prayed. Not only did he pray, but he also kept praying. His prayers were short, repetitive, frank and desperate. He prayed the same thing three times and yet, in the end, there was no apparent effect. Were Jesus' prayers in Gethsemane futile?

In life, even when we pray earnestly and repeatedly, God often remains silent without granting what we ask for. Often our complaint is exactly this: "I kept praying and praying, but I don't see any result!" After Jesus' first prayer, he still struggled, so he prayed the second time, saying the same prayer. After the second prayer, he was still struggling. He prayed the third time, still saying the same prayer as before. Notice that Scripture emphasizes that the content of his three prayers was exactly the same (verse 44). In other words, Jesus didn't seem to make any progress even after praying. Scripture seems to suggest that Jesus' prayers didn't yield any results. Just like us, he was still weak, still stressed, and still at 'square one' after praying. There was no breakthrough and no answer to his struggles and pain. We all have had this experience, and it turns out Jesus had the same experience too.

So what is the point of prayer if it doesn't seem to work?

Prayer is not about results, rewards, solutions or turning the tide of luck. It is to help us align our hearts with God's heart, to correct our vision, perspectives and mindset. When we are tuned in to God's frequency, we will naturally discern what God's will is. However, though the soul is willing, the body is weak. Jesus clearly saw his struggle and he tuned his perspective every time he prayed: "However, don't do what I want, just do what you want" (Verse 39). Every time he prayed, he let go of his personal will and became more sensitive to and in sync with God's will. Prayers open up the space where we examine our inner condition and reflect on the sources of our emotions and reactions. Tune your heart to God's heart, this is how Jesus prayed in the Garden of Gethsemane. As we keep praying, we keep adjusting.

Therefore, another valuable lesson we can learn from Jesus' prayers is that we don't have to wait until everything is in order before we can seek God through prayer. Even if you clearly know that you are not yet fully ready to submit to His will, at least not physically or emotionally, you can still present this incompleteness to God, as long as you continue to pray.

However, when it comes to prayer, we are always full of excuses:

"Oh, I'm weak and can't get motivated!"

"I'm so busy, how can I find time?"

"I'm so tired I fall asleep as soon as I pray"...

How *can* we pray? Scripture does not tell us to learn *how* to pray, but that we *need* to pray. The busier we are, the more tired we are, the weaker we are, the more broken we feel, the more we need to pray! This is exactly how Jesus is different from us.

When Jesus was saying to his disciples, "Your spirit is willing, but your flesh is weak" (verse 41), he is not reproaching them, because when he said this, he himself was also at the weakest point in his own life. Jesus understands you at your lowest point, for he has been there. The Bible says that he can truly sympathize with our weaknesses because he "has been tempted in everything, just like us" (Hebrews 4:15). Among all the religions in the world, only the God of Christianity is willing to become as helpless as a man and suffer to the point of death like a man, because He came to bring life to the hurting and the weak.

When you want to be willing, but you are not willing

Have you wondered why Jesus went to the Garden of Gethsemane that night? We know that Judas had long known that the place was the meeting point of Jesus and his disciples (John 18:2). After Jesus suggested that Judas go out to accomplish his plan, he and his disciples went to Gethsemane. In other words, Jesus went there waiting to be captured. If Jesus was truly unwilling, he would have been hiding elsewhere, far from the garden, so that no one could find him. However, Jesus went there knowing that was where he would be found, and that was when he experienced sorrow to the point of death.

At times, the fact that you are struggling already indicates that you are willing. John Wilbur Chapman, an American revival evangelist and pastor in the 19th century, made many sacrifices for serving the Lord when he was young. Yet one day, the toll of his ministries caught up with him and he began to plunge into deep despair and wariness as the ongoing discouragement left him dejected and wanting to give up. It so happened that F. B. Meyer came to lead a revival meeting where he was. Hoping to give himself another chance to continue serving, he decided to go and listen to Meyer. Meyer asked a question that would alter Chapman's life, "If you are not willing to give up everything for Christ, are you willing to be made willing?" To that question Chapman replied, "I am willing to let God make me willing." Chapman later became one of the greatest evangelists in 19th century America.

DARKEST NIGHT, BRIGHTEST DAWN: A LENT REFLECTION

When we cry out to God, "Lord, I'm not too willing", we are finally inviting God to do His work in us and empower us to be willing to do His will. Jesus' situation in the Garden of Gethsemane showed us that this is the way. In the face of immense struggles and weaknesses, he asked God to make him willing. Are we willing to let God make us willing? It has been said that in any revival of the church or individual, three things are indispensable: first, prayer; second, prayer; third, more prayer. Like Jesus' way in the Garden of Gethsemane, our only way is to keep praying. Jesus faced struggles just like we do. Hebrews 5:7-8 tells us:

> 7 During the days of Jesus' life on earth, he offered up prayers and petitions with fervent cries and tears to the one who could save him from death, and he was heard because of his reverent submission. 8 Son though he was, he learned obedience from what he suffered 9 and, once made perfect, he became the source of eternal salvation for all who obey him.

In fact, Jesus' short and desperate prayers were answered. He answered his Father's call, enduring to the end with complete obedience that triumphed over death. The Good News not only lies in this final victory, but also in Jesus' journey from weakness to victory through prayer.

Reflection and Response

1. Does the story change the way you look at weakness and prayer? How so?
2. Why do you think Jesus addressed the issue of 'The spirit is willing but the flesh is weak' before he went onto the cross?
3. What can we do when our flesh is weak?
4. Is there any area in your life you are unwilling to submit to God? Are you willing to be made willing?

Broken

.

(John 18:1-11)

.

The journey of soul-searching at Lent is both heavy and uplifting. We see the ugliness and hopelessness of human sin, but we also find unconditional acceptance and love from Jesus because he is determined to love us to the very end (Chapter 1). In the face of our human weaknesses, we are also assured to find full understanding and identification in Jesus, because he has personally been through the same struggles (Chapter 2). Yet every day we still face the same strains and brokenness in life battering us with discouragement. No one is free from troubles and trials. Even in Jesus' life, these couldn't be avoided. In the Garden of Gethsemane, again, what we can see in Jesus' example is how unmeasurable mercy and assurance from above is the answer to all fears.

Let's dive into John 18. First, focus on the first four verses:

> **1** When he had finished praying, Jesus left with his disciples and crossed the Kidron Valley. On the other side there was a garden, and he and his disciples went into it.

2 Now Judas, who betrayed him, knew the place, because Jesus had often met there with his disciples. **3** So Judas came to the garden, guiding a detachment of soldiers and some officials from the chief priests and the Pharisees. They were carrying torches, lanterns and weapons.

4 Jesus, knowing all that was going to happen to him, went out and asked them, "Who is it you want?"

The passage highlights one verb twice: "to know". What is there to know? The first 'know' appears in verse 2, referring to Judas. The Garden of Gethsemane was where Jesus and his disciples used to go to pray regularly. During the time of Passover, it was the custom for families to travel to Jerusalem and stay there for several days to observe the religious festival, but the city of Jerusalem itself could not provide accommodation for the whole Jewish population, so people would often stay temporarily in the suburbs surrounding Jerusalem. Yet people would not go any further than the suburbs, or it would be too much commuting. This was why Jesus still returned to Jerusalem every night to spend the night in the Garden of Gethsemane under the Mount of Olives on the outskirts of the city.

Indeed, having spent much intimate time with Jesus over three years, Judas was familiar with the routines of Jesus and his disciples, and he 'knew' very well that the best time to betray the Lord was when Jesus was in Gethsemane at night because the chief priests had said not to arrest Jesus in broad daylight and not to cause a disturbance. No one was following Jesus late at night, so that would be a good opportunity to arrest him.

The whole setup

Perhaps Judas was too confident in thinking that he was the only one who knew what was happening that night. He was the one who 'set it up', but the second "to know", of course, belongs to Jesus. It was Jesus who truly knew the real 'setup' for that evening. John emphasizes that it was Jesus who took the initiative to instruct Judas to go and do what he had planned (John 13:27). So even though on the surface, the story looks like it was Judas who planned to betray Jesus in a surprise attack, in reality it was Jesus' plan that overrode all other plans. Jesus could have stopped Judas or escaped his capture, yet he chose to come to the Garden of Gethsemane early and wait for Judas' gang to arrive and be arrested by them.

Have you ever played chess with someone who is really good at it? The chess master always thinks in advance and has the end game in mind. If you don't know their plans, you may only see their individual moves one by one. They, however, see the whole big picture and slowly lead you to their setup step by step. Their early moves didn't seem to make sense until suddenly, it's checkmate!

In your life, who is in control of the whole 'setup'? Who truly knows the path you are taking? Whose plans override all other plans in the end? Once you figure out the answers to these questions, everything in your life has a totally different purpose and meaning. Other people, no matter whether it's your parents, your boss or your enemies, might have tried to set up your life for you with their own schemes. Yet only God's scheme defines your life. In other words, you are never trapped or hopeless if God is the one planning your life. Neither was Jesus. Jesus was not technically betrayed or trapped because God's masterplan was the one that was truly unfolding. God knows, and only God knows, the bigger picture behind all the troubles and brokenness that are making you weary right now.

We see numerous examples like this throughout the Bible. Moses' ambition was to save his people from Egypt and yet, when he tried to save one Hebrew man, even his own people betrayed him (Exodus 2). He ended up fleeing and wandering in the wilderness for 40 years, discouraged and battered. Little did he know that all these small and seemingly pointless experiences were part of God's masterplan to prepare him for the great exodus 40 years later. It was only when Moses looked back with hindsight that he saw that every single detail in the early stages of his life was part of God's bigger purpose. God is always working, even when we can't see him working.

This is the same in our lives. What is happening right in front of our eyes is not the most important. What God is planning behind the scenes is what truly matters. Of course, you might say, knowing God is in charge of His bigger plans does not make life any easier when we are still living in hardship and pain every day. True. But we must remember that God never downplays or dismisses suffering.

Let's continue reading the story:

> **4** Jesus, knowing all that was going to happen to him, went out and asked them, "Who is it you want?"

5 "Jesus of Nazareth," they replied.

"I am he," Jesus said. (And Judas the traitor was standing there with them.) **6** When Jesus said, "I am he," they drew back and fell to the ground.

7 Again he asked them, "Who is it you want?"

"Jesus of Nazareth," they said.

8 Jesus answered, "I told you that I am he. If you are looking for me, then let these men go." **9** This happened so that the words he had spoken would be fulfilled: "I have not lost one of those you gave me."

While the previous part of the story highlights the verb "to know" twice, this section highlights the question "Who are you looking for?" twice, as if Jesus wanted to make sure that they got the right person and make things easier for them.

The soldiers were ordered to arrest Jesus, but they seemed a little confused in how to identify him. Perhaps Judas still hadn't given the sign of the kiss yet. Perhaps it was very dark. Notice the passage emphasizes that Jesus already knew all the suffering and pain ahead, and he was the one who asked the question, "Who is it you are looking for?" to face the suffering head on.

What's in a name?

When they said, "Jesus of Nazareth," Jesus replied, "I AM" and instantly, the men backed away and fell to the ground. What a scene! Indeed, the answer "I AM" was not only stating the fact that they had caught the right guy. Anyone familiar with Judaism knew very well it was much more than that. It is the unique name for God Himself. In Exodus 3, when God called Moses to bring His people out of Egypt, Moses was hesitant and afraid, asking for reassurance from God:

> "Suppose I go to the Israelites and say to them, 'The God of your fathers has sent me to you,' and they ask me, 'What is his name?' Then what shall I tell them?" God answered, "I am who I am. This is what you are to say to the Israelites: 'I AM has sent me to you.'" (Exodus 3:13-14)

Why does God call Himself "I AM"? He is the one who was, who is, and who is to come. God's identity doesn't need any more clarification. The plainness and lucidity of the name suggests God does not need to use any term to explain Himself, and He is exactly who He says He is. Moses had a full guarantee from God that He would be with him when God called him to tell Pharaoh to "let my people go". This was the essence of Jesus' reply when he presented himself as "I AM".

In fact, John, the author, intentionally uses the same word multiple times in his writing: "I am the bread of life" (6:35), "I am the light of the world" (8:12), "I am the way, the truth and the life" (14:6). These are all titles and claims exclusive to God.

But also notice what Jesus said next and John's careful explanation:

Jesus answered, "I told you that I am he. If you are looking for me, then let these men go." This happened so that the words he had spoken would be fulfilled: "I have not lost one of those you gave me. (verses 8-9)

In other words, the name "I AM" is not only about power and authority. It also carries a guarantee of salvation and liberation for all those who belong to God. Just like in the context of Exodus 3, God was not just coming up with a fancy name to make Himself sound cool in front of Pharaoh. Nor was it only to make people scared (although we should tremble with fear before God). The name was a firm promise that He would accomplish what He said he would: to deliver all His people out of the hands of Pharaoh. If He said it, He would do it. 100%.

As Jesus identified himself with a name exclusive to God, he declared he would fulfil all of the promises God has made in Scripture. It is a guarantee of absolute authority and absolute faithfulness that not one of us will be lost. In this most terrifying and darkest moment in the Garden of Gethsemane, there is nothing to fear. The only one we should fear is Jesus himself, and in Jesus we can find full assurance of God's salvation. The one who has promised to be with us always is also the one who is faithful. Not one will be lost, including you and me.

Fighting in our own way

The story, however, got more tense and violent, not because of Jesus but because of Peter:

9 This happened so that the words he had spoken would be fulfilled: "I have not lost one of those you gave me."

10 Then Simon Peter, who had a sword, drew it and struck the high priest's servant, cutting off his right ear. (The servant's name was Malchus.)

11 Jesus commanded Peter, "Put your sword away! Shall I not drink the cup the Father has given me?"

Confused and scared, Peter impulsively drew his sword and cut off the right ear of one of the high priest's servants, Malchus. John chooses to mention Malchus by name possibly because he later became a follower of Jesus and was known to the disciples. But have you ever wondered why Scripture recorded which ear Peter struck off? Why the right ear? Some commentators believe Peter might have been left-handed. Well, we don't know for sure, but perhaps a better explanation is that Peter struck Malchus from the back, as he was probably unable or too scared to do it from the front.

In the face of threat and unexpected crisis, Peter was simply overwhelmed by the threat that seemingly appeared from nowhere. He had no idea what God had planned for that evening and how all these commotions fitted into God's glorious redemption blueprint. Guided by his emotions and relying on his blind understanding and resources, he quickly resorted to his own method of defending himself. He thought he was doing Jesus a big favour by protecting him; little did he know that he was meddling with God's biggest plan in human history.

DARKEST NIGHT, BRIGHTEST DAWN: A LENT REFLECTION

Jesus didn't command Judas' gang to back off. Instead, Jesus ordered Peter to put down his sword. His weapon is redundant, self-centred, and a stumbling block to God's plan. Was Jesus instructing Peter to surrender to Judas? No, not at all, but he was leading him to surrender to Jesus himself and to allow him to lead the way. God never calls us to submit to our enemies and give up. He calls us to surrender to Him and to let Him take charge.

Now notice another verb that is highlighted twice in the passage: "to give". Both instances refer to what God has given Jesus: the first one is the people God has given to Jesus, and the second one is the 'cup', the cup of suffering which Jesus accepted in obedience to the Father. In Scripture the notion of 'cup' often refers to the portion God has given to each one of us in our lives. What Jesus was going through was from the Father above. To accept it means to say to the Father, "not my will, but yours, be done."

We have seen previously that although Judas had betrayed Jesus, Jesus was not passively betrayed, because he was fully aware and in charge of all the events unfolding. Now we also see how Jesus was not being overcome or defeated by Judas, because he chose to surrender to God's will and did not lose anyone who belonged to him.

Looking back on my own life, I remember I was once a young man full of anxiety and fear. My mind would be full of wariness of what misfortune might happen to me or what people thought of me. But as I slowly grew in my walk with God, one of the biggest lessons I have learned in life is this: when I truly fear God, then I have nothing else to fear in life. In the Garden of Gethsemane, Jesus appeared to be a 'struggler' as he also had to wrestle with the same human brokenness our world is struggling with, but in fact, he was the real commander of the story. Not only that, today he is still the same commander who loves unconditionally to the end, so that under him we can all face our shame and darkness with boldness. We don't surrender to the troubles and sorrows of this world, but we need to surrender totally to our Creator who has called us to live the abundant life He has prepared for us.

Reflection and Response

1. Who do you think determines the whole 'setup' of your life? How does this belief shape the way you live every day?

2. What does God's name "I AM" mean to you?

3. When confronted with a crisis in the Garden of Gethsemane, Peter quickly drew his weapon and struck off the high priest's servant's right ear. In what ways are we like Peter?

4. When we live through the darkest hours of life, how do Jesus' answers to Peter's action and to his enemies' capture in Gethsemane help us face our Gethsemane?

Condemned

·

(John 18:18-19:16)

·

L ent often opens up a time for deep introspection. When reading the final chapters of the four Gospels, we often love to jump quickly to the happy finale when Jesus rose from the dead. Knowing there is a hopeful ending is important, but Scripture records many details of Jesus' journey from Gethsemane to the trial and from the trial to his death on the cross because these details give us invaluable lessons on what it really means to follow Jesus. I will divide this part into two chapters to discuss this epiphany with you. This chapter reflects on why Jesus had to die on a cross, and the next chapter examines the journey of Jesus' death.

So why did Jesus die? Christians know the proper answer to this question off by heart: because we are sinful and the wage of sin is death, but God loves us so much that He sent His son Jesus Christ to die on the cross in our place. And so on. We are all familiar with this answer. It sounds simple and straightforward, but if you really think about it, there is absolutely nothing simple about this explanation.

First, if we say that Jesus is God, then he can't really die. How could it be possible for God to be given the death penalty? The Messiah God had promised the world would himself carry all our guilt and be sacrificed for our sins. This means he must die—but how can God *die*? Second, in order to be sentenced to death for our sins, Jesus must be condemned first, but Jesus himself is without sin, so then someone would have to find a way to charge and condemn him with something.

However, on the other hand, if Jesus is declared guilty, then he would only be dying for his own guilt and therefore by no means dying for the sins of the world. He would just be another convicted criminal among many others in history. In other words, if Jesus is the legitimate Messiah, Saviour, the Lamb of God, then he must be officially declared innocent while also officially condemned and sentenced to death *at the same time*. This is ridiculous and practically impossible in any functional legal court. Only God could orchestrate the events on the first Good Friday to make this impossible scenario possible.

Can a court declare someone innocent and sentence him to death at the same time?

The Gospel authors tried very hard to present how both of these mutually impossible scenarios astonishingly took place at the same time in Jesus' trial. It all converged on one historical figure: the Roman governor, Pontius Pilate. Pilate's role was so pivotal that even the Apostles' Creed deliberately mentions him by his full name, stating that Jesus "suffered under Pontius Pilate, was crucified, died, and was buried."

How did it all happen? Let's look first at John 18:28-29.

> **28** Then the Jewish leaders took Jesus from Caiaphas to the palace of the Roman governor. By now it was early morning, and to avoid ceremonial uncleanness they did not enter the palace, because they wanted to be able to eat the Passover. **29** So Pilate came out to them and asked, "What charges are you bringing against this man?"

For the people who arrested Jesus in the Garden of Gethsemane, their troublesome evening had only just begun. It was dawn, very early in the morning, most likely it was still dark, when the people took Jesus into the Roman governor's palace (the Praetorium). Yet they didn't enter it, because stepping foot in it would make them unclean, which would mean they couldn't participate in the Passover feast. This was why Pilate went out to meet them and asked, "What are you accusing this man of?"

Another problem they encountered was the fact that they could not kill Jesus legally. As subjects under Roman rule, the Jews had no right to sentence anyone to death. So they had no choice but to bring Jesus to the Roman authorities, their worst enemies, for trial, almost begging Pilate to carry out the death sentence for them. The entire scenario was absurd and embarrassing for the Jewish leaders who saw Jesus, one of their own people, as a bigger enemy than the Romans.

To make things trickier, they had to do this around 6 am in the morning in order to finish the whole process before Passover officially started, when everyone had to head home to prepare for the big feast. It was so early that they probably even had to wake up the Roman officials to handle the matter. In addition, it was almost impossible to convince the Romans to take the case, especially when the charge was rather ambiguous and awkward. Pilate did not refuse, however, probably because he wanted to please the Jews or did not want to cause trouble with them.

Under whose law should Jesus be tried?

Now we witness an intriguing conversation between Pilate and the Jewish leaders. Yet notice how this bizarre trial and complex power-struggle essentially fulfilled everything that Scripture had prophesied about the Lamb of God, revealing that it was God who really coordinated the whole historical chain of events that evening.

Pilate asked, "What are you accusing this man of?" They replied, "If this man was not a wicked man, we would not hand him over to you" (verse 30). They did not answer his question at all.

Since the court had not yet officially opened at that time, Pilate came out to reason with them. The first issue Pilate had to deal with was to define and classify this rather unusual case, and to figure out under whose jurisdiction the case should be handled. Was it a civil or a criminal case? Was it a Jewish internal matter or a national matter? If this was to be a civil case, then the Jews were to conduct the trial themselves, but there would be no death penalty. Yet if it was to be a criminal case, then capital punishment would be possible, but it would need to be tried by Pilate. This crucial question of jurisdiction and authority must be dealt with first.

In order to put Jesus to death, the Jewish leaders must convince the Romans to accept the case, and this was only their first problem. The second problem was to define what exactly the charge was. Notice that in the beginning the Jews did not say what crime Jesus had committed. The most obvious reason was because Jesus had not done anything wrong. The other, more disconcerting, reason was simply the fact that they wanted Jesus dead precisely because he claimed to be the Messiah, and they had always been waiting for their own 'messiah' to overthrow the Romans for them. How ironic. Now they had to risk being the Romans' laughingstock for bringing one of their own people to the Romans for trial and begging the governor to do a favour for them by putting him to death.

Pilate's stance was clear from the start. He said, "Take him yourselves, and ask him according to your law" (verse 30). As far as Pilate was concerned, this case was not his business at all and he would rather just stay out of it. But the Jews insisted, "We have no authority to kill" (verse 31).

Scripture then explains that this was to fulfil what Jesus had said about the kind of death he would die (verse 32). Earlier, in John 12:32, Jesus had mentioned specifically how he would die: "And I, when I am lifted up from the earth, will draw all people to myself." So, Jesus had already stated that he would be lifted up, that is, he would die on a cross. If the Jews were to carry out an execution under their own law, they could only stone the person to death according to the Law of Moses. Only the Roman authorities could torture and crucify the criminal on a 'tree' (cross). In other words, the way God intended the Messiah to die was beyond the Jewish leaders' scheming. God was intervening to make this possible.

We often say that Jesus is the Lord of Life, but here we see in fact he is the Lord of Death as well. He had total control over how and when he died. Jesus died, not because he was framed or betrayed: he had already stated how he would die in order to fulfil Scripture. The entire evening went in the exact direction that could fulfil all the prophecies and requirements of the sacrifice God had intended.

Did the Messiah really need to die on a cross?

Have you wondered why Jesus chose the way of the cross? Wouldn't other causes of death be better options? A heart attack would have been nice and less messy. Could Jesus have died for the sins of the world by a less painful death? Was it to achieve maximum suffering in order to show God's greatest love? Or was there more to this?

It is important to explain this in the context of Hebrew Scripture. It was stated that "everyone who hangs on a tree is cursed" (Galatians 3:13; see Deuteronomy 21:22-23), and Jesus chose the death penalty of being hung on a tree because it was the ultimate curse for sin. But why? Because sin must be cursed. The third chapter of Genesis tells us clearly that after Adam and Eve sinned against God, the first thing God pronounced was a curse. However, the curse was not against Adam and Eve, but against the Serpent (Genesis 3:14).

Yet notice how God dealt with Adam and Eve next. God declared the consequence of their sin: pain and hardships in giving birth and cultivating the land. Since the very beginning, in Genesis 1, being fruitful in multiplying and enjoying the fruits of the land were both direct representations of God's blessings for mankind. Even when man sinned against God, God was determined to continue His blessings and never to curse mankind. In order to make this possible, God chose to take the curse upon Himself. The significance of Jesus dying on the cross is that God Himself would rather become the object of the curse for the sins of man. To tangibly demonstrate and fulfil this, he chose to be lifted up and hung on a tree—the cross.

Whose jurisdiction? Whose King is Jesus?

Now it was Pilate's turn to speak to Jesus. He immediately found himself in the middle of a thorny conundrum: what crime should Jesus be charged with so that he could have the death sentence which the Jewish leaders were demanding? When "Pilate went back inside the palace" (verse 33), it meant that the case was officially accepted and put on trial. As Jesus was brought in, Pilate asked him, "Are you the king of the Jews?" This was the only accusation against Jesus that the accusers could come up with. At that time, the Jews were under the rule of the Roman Empire and the Romans were paranoid about the possibility of an uprising. There was no way the Romans would allow the Jews to have their own king. If Jesus was the king of the Jews, it would imply he intended to rebel against the Romans. Only by accusing Jesus of treason at the highest level would his case have a chance to carry the highest penalty—death.

Pilate had no choice but to ask Jesus: "Is this charge against you true?" Jesus responded, "Did you say this yourself, or did someone else say it to you about me?" (verse 34). Jesus flipped the table and challenged the authority behind Pilate's questioning and the trial itself.

If it was the Romans who accused Jesus, it would have made much more sense. Now the Jews were accusing one of their own people, so Pilate knew very well that they were just trying to get rid of Jesus out of jealousy (Matt. 27:183, Mark 15:10). After all, this accusation from the Jews was absurd. Judging from Jesus' question, Pilate was more certain that he was not guilty of having violated any Roman law.

The trial continued:

> **35** "Am I a Jew?" Pilate replied. "Your own people and chief priests handed you over to me. What is it you have done?"

> **36** Jesus said, "My kingdom is not of this world. If it were, my servants would fight to prevent my arrest by the Jewish leaders. But now my kingdom is from another place."

If there had been a real rebellion, the people who hated the Romans wouldn't have arrested their own leader and handed him over to the authorities, and besides, the Romans would have dealt with it a long time ago without the help of Judas. Pilate knew there was something much more to it but had no clue what it was.

So Jesus gave Pilate some hints: his kingdom is not the kingdom of the world. Jesus' power was not to be understood in human terms, neither in Jewish terms nor by Roman law. His authority extends far beyond this world, beyond all politics and human hierarchies. Even then Pilate still didn't understand. He remarked,

> **37** "You are a king, then!" said Pilate.
>
> Jesus answered, "You say that I am a king. In fact, the reason I was born and came into the world is to testify to the truth. Everyone on the side of truth listens to me."
>
> **38** "What is truth?" retorted Pilate. With this he went out again to the Jews gathered there and said, "I find no basis for a charge against him. **39** But it is your custom for me to release to you one prisoner at the time of the Passover. Do you want me to release 'the king of the Jews'?"

Jesus is not only the King of Life and the King of Death, but also the King of Truth. Truth is the ultimate standard under which everything in this world is to be understood, judged and defined. When Jesus becomes King in our lives, he is not an adviser or a consultant, he becomes the ultimate ruler. You cannot invite Jesus as King without having all your standards, values and perspectives totally overturned.

Putting TRUTH on trial

So now Pilate and the people were essentially trying to put Truth on trial. The irony is that it should be the other way round. All trials are conducted to reveal the truth and all things are measured against the truth. So how can Truth be guilty? If you put Truth on trial, then by what standards and measurements are you using to reach your verdict? Truth cannot be guilty. Why would people want to accuse Truth and condemn Truth to death? The answer is obvious: because we find Truth highly offensive, inconvenient and threatening, we want to create our own 'truth' that fits our world; we don't want *the* Truth.

When Pilate asked, "What is truth?", he was not seeking some metaphysical or epistemological discussion. Seeing the Jews' desperate attempt to get rid of Jesus but unable to come up with a convincing charge, Pilate is hoping to finish the trial off quickly and get out of this difficult case ASAP. He had already reached his verdict: Jesus was innocent. In fact, he repeated his verdict clearly three times, "I can't find any fault in this man" (18:38, 19: 4-6).

However, the mob was totally fixated on killing Jesus despite Pilate's non-guilty verdict. As the story unfolds, we see Pilate trying to appease the crowd in three different ways.

How far would you go to nail Jesus on the cross?

First, Pilate tried to play along with the Jewish festive atmosphere that morning (verse 39). All his Jewish subjects were busy preparing for a big feast and anticipating the biggest religious celebration of the year. Why ruin the festivity with a death sentence? If one of the holiday traditions was to pardon a prisoner, then wouldn't it be a great opportunity to pardon the one standing right in front of them? Jesus was labelled 'King of the Jews' after all. Why not release the 'King of the Jews' in a Jewish festival? How convenient. Of course not. This trick didn't work on the people whose biggest goal of that Passover was to slaughter Jesus: "No, not him! Give us Barabbas!" (verse 40).

Pilate now had to think of a second strategy. He tried to satisfy the angry mob by having Jesus severely beaten and mocked in public. If these people hate Jesus so much, Pilate thought, they should be satisfied by watching Jesus suffer under torture and publicly humiliated. Under the Romans, there were three levels of physical torture. The first, lighter level, was a less severe form of beating and humiliation, which was what was happening here (the second level would be after the guilty verdict). Perhaps the people would accept this flogging as the punishment they had always wanted for Jesus? This was also a great opportunity for Pilate's own political career as he now had a chance to humiliate one of his Jewish subjects (the title 'King of the Jews' would have been a comical charge during this occasion), thus displaying his authority in front of his subjects and the Roman Emperor's power in public. Yet this method didn't work either. The people only had one thing in their mind: to crucify Jesus.

Finally, Pilate tried to get out of trouble by simply asking the people to crucify Jesus themselves, "You take him and crucify him. As for me, I find no basis for a charge against him" (19:6). If you can't exchange the prisoner or the sentence, then perhaps you can try exchanging the executioner? Matthew specifically tells us Pilate emphasized his freedom from responsibility by washing his hands in front of the crowd, thinking he could finally leave the matter behind and get on with life. Little did he know the people's next response would make him tremble.

> 7 The Jewish leaders insisted, "We have a law, and according to that law he must die, because he claimed to be the Son of God."

> 8 When Pilate heard this, he was even more afraid, 9 and he went back inside the palace. "Where do you come from?" he asked Jesus, but Jesus gave him no answer.

This final statement introduced a new accusation against Jesus on a totally new level: Jesus claimed to be the Son of God. Pilate realized that things were not as simple as he had thought. The religious leaders were not getting rid of Jesus purely out of jealousy of his popularity. There was a spiritual dimension to this trial—Jesus claimed to be divine. The contemporary Greco-Roman culture had many forms of superstitions and worship of different gods. No religious matters were taken lightly. We don't know much about Pilate's personal beliefs, but he certainly understood the seriousness of the matter. He realised that what he was dealing with was not a political issue but something beyond him. Now he was scared.

Pilate's first reaction was fear. He immediately interrogated Jesus again, "Where are you from? Who are you? Are you human, or are you really God?" The new round of questions now belonged to a higher realm beyond Pilate's own, and he couldn't help but panic. To his frustration, this time Jesus didn't say a word. So why didn't Jesus respond? He answered all of Pilate's previous questions. According to the law at the time, if the defendant did not give an answer, he would imply he accepted the accusation.

Pilate's earlier questions were all about the nature of the criminal charge, to which Jesus could not confess because he was not guilty. However, this time it wasn't about any charge; it was about who Jesus really was, his true identity, which Jesus had already answered. What Jesus really meant by refusing to answer was, "I'm not answerable to you. You are answerable to me, for I'm the King."

We can perhaps feel a little sympathy for Pilate. Imagine the anger and frustration exploding inside of him. First, he was woken up before dawn to take on this strange case that was none of his business. After trying to be nice to the Jews and giving in to their demands, Pilate conducted the trial and finally came up with the verdict that Jesus was not guilty, but it wasn't accepted by the mob! Now when he realized the accusation contained an unexpected religious twist, he tried to get more information from the defendant, only to find that he suddenly refused to talk! Now he's stuck in between.

The judge had become more anxious than the defendant.

> **10** "Do you refuse to speak to me?" Pilate said. "Don't you realize I have power either to free you or to crucify you?"

11 Jesus answered, "You would have no power over me if it were not given to you from above. Therefore the one who handed me over to you is guilty of a greater sin."

The crux of the case was who had the real authority to judge and condemn. Jesus pointed out to Pilate who the ultimate judge was—God. If God had not allowed him to take this position of governor for now, he would have had no chance to question Jesus at all. The seat of the judge should have been taken by Jesus. Indeed, Pilate was trapped in multiple dilemmas, both political and legal, and now even religious ones. Then, the final straw came. Verse 12 tells us the Jewish leaders cried out,

"If you release this man, you are not a loyal servant of Caesar." Whoever makes himself king has betrayed Caesar."

When the judge became the defendant

The religious leaders' last resort finally worked. The tipping point was when Pilate realised that he himself was implicated directly in his own verdict and sentencing. Since Jesus was a potential traitor to the Roman authorities (at least according to the accusers), if Pilate released Jesus, then he would also be a traitor! The people were basically saying: "Even we are loyal to Caesar. How dare you betray Caesar, Pilate?"

What a great political manoeuvre. Suddenly, Pilate realised he was the one who had to defend and save himself. It turned out both the Jews and Pilate felt threatened by Jesus.

13 When Pilate heard this, he brought Jesus out and sat down on the judge's seat at a place known as the Stone Pavement (which in Aramaic is Gabbatha). **14** It was the day of Preparation of the Passover; it was about noon.

"Here is your king," Pilate said to the Jews.

15 But they shouted, "Take him away! Take him away! Crucify him!"

"Shall I crucify your king?" Pilate asked.

"We have no king but Caesar," the chief priests answered.

16 Finally Pilate handed him over to them to be crucified.

Here is the end of a spectacular political wrestling match. While the Jewish leaders used Pilate to eliminate Jesus, Pilate also used Jesus to ridicule the Jews. Yet in the end, it was God who orchestrated every detail of the whole situation to have Pilate declare Jesus was innocent while sentencing him to the cross, thus fulfilling His plan of the perfect sacrifice He had prepared for the world.

Have you reached your verdict?

This is worth pondering: Jesus is the King, he is the King of Life, the King of Death, and he is also the King of Truth. Both the Jewish leaders and Pilate were faced with the momentous task of figuring out what they wanted to do with this King. What about us? How would we want to treat this king?

The Jewish people have always had a strong national consciousness, but this time they would rather sacrifice their dignity, give up their national pride, and risk political embarrassment in order to use the Romans' power to get rid of Jesus. Pilate, on the other hand, also buried his conscience. He had found Jesus innocent but was unprepared to offend the crowd or put his political career at risk. Saving his own face and proving his loyalty to Caesar had a higher priority than following the truth, and he finally gave in and had Jesus crucified.

We, too, are faced with the same momentous decision today. Whether we choose to hail Jesus as King or to crucify him on a cross, the cost is high. What is our verdict, and how far are we willing to go to uphold our decision?

Reflection and Response

1. The Gospel tells us that Jesus took upon himself the curse of sin that we all deserve. What does his trial before Pilate reveal to us about the nature of sin and God's salvation?

2. Pilate asked Jesus many profound questions throughout the trial, but in the end, he chose to submit to the crowd's demands rather than to Jesus' claims. In what ways are we like Pilate?

3. "When Jesus becomes King in our lives, he is not an adviser or a consultant, he becomes the ultimate ruler." Is Jesus the ultimate ruler of your life or just an adviser?

4. Jesus said, "My kingdom is not of this world." How is this manifested as we live in this world as disciples of Jesus?

Dying

.

(John 19:28-37)

.

28 Later, knowing that everything had now been finished, and so that Scripture would be fulfilled, Jesus said, "I am thirsty." **29** A jar of wine vinegar was there, so they soaked a sponge in it, put the sponge on a stalk of the hyssop plant, and lifted it to Jesus' lips. **30** When he had received the drink, Jesus said, "It is finished." With that, he bowed his head and gave up his spirit.

31 Now it was the day of Preparation, and the next day was to be a special Sabbath. Because the Jewish leaders did not want the bodies left on the crosses during the Sabbath, they asked Pilate to have the legs broken and the bodies taken down. **32** The soldiers therefore came and broke the legs of the first man who had been crucified with Jesus, and then those of the other. **33** But when they came to Jesus and found that he was already dead, they did not break his legs. **34** Instead, one of the soldiers pierced

Jesus' side with a spear, bringing a sudden flow of blood and water. **35** The man who saw it has given testimony, and his testimony is true. He knows that he tells the truth, and he testifies so that you also may believe. **36** These things happened so that the scripture would be fulfilled: "Not one of his bones will be broken," **37**and, as another scripture says, "They will look on the one they have pierced."

As our journey of reflection on the Passion of Christ continues, we now enter the most difficult part of it: Jesus' death on the cross. We have already seen in the previous chapter how the declaration of Jesus' innocence and his death sentence occurred at the same time to fulfil Scripture. Looking closely now at the process of Jesus' death brings us two important reflections: one is his love and the other is the absolute assurance of who Jesus is. The former is often highlighted when we remember Good Friday and celebrate Easter, but not always the latter.

As we remember Jesus' death, I will focus primarily on what he said just before he died. Scripture records Jesus making seven different statements while he was on the cross, three of which are found in John, Chapter 19.

Why should we look at what he said on the cross? None of us has ever been physically nailed and suspended on a piece of wood. But we can imagine the unspeakable pain Jesus must have endured as he hung there. He would also have great difficulty even breathing, let alone speaking. When Jesus' limbs were pierced by giant nails and the sheer weight of his body hung on those nails, he had to muster what little remaining strength he had just to raise his body enough to take in one breath. No one would want to say anything in this situation unless it was absolutely necessary, so we know what Jesus said on the cross must be highly important.

"I thirst."

It is not surprising that all statements made by Jesus in John's narratives were very short. In fact, in the original text, two of the three statements were only made up of one word. The first word Διψῶ (Dipsō) (I thirst) can be found in verses 28:

> **28** Later, knowing that everything had now been finished, and so that Scripture would be fulfilled, Jesus said, "I am thirsty." **29** A jar of wine vinegar was there, so they soaked a sponge in it, put the sponge on a stalk of the hyssop plant, and lifted it to Jesus' lips.

"I am thirsty"—What a shocking statement coming from Jesus himself. Dehydration is expected as part of the horrific suffering anyone who is crucified would go through. We know someone brought a sponge soaked with vinegar to Jesus' mouth. Why was this significant? The passage clearly implied that the vinegar was not something that had been prepared for Jesus earlier but was given to him on the spur of the moment, but why? Vinegar might quench his thirst and thus revive him for a little while, but no one would give vinegar to someone who was being crucified because it would only prolong the agonising pain. No one being nailed on a cross would want to live longer.

However, the vinegar mentioned here is not to be confused with the wine mixed with myrrh mentioned in the Gospel of Mark (Mark 15:23). Alcohol has analgesic effects and can relieve pain. People prepared wine for Jesus instead of vinegar, but according to Mark, Jesus refused to drink the wine. Instead, he deliberately chose to take the vinegar that others would have refused, in order to fulfil the words of Scripture.

How many ancient prophecies can you fulfil in one afternoon?

In verse 28, the word "finished" means fulfilled and completed. It is the same word Τετέλεσται (Tetelestai) later used in verse 30, "It is finished". By now we can see all four Gospel accounts of Jesus' crucifixion repetitively emphasize the fact that each detail in his death fulfilled the Hebrew Scriptures.

Matthew records another famous statement made by Jesus on the cross, "My God! My God! Why have you forsaken me?" (Matthew 27:46). Although he didn't indicate the source of the quote, the author deliberately kept the Aramaic expression Jesus originally used and then added the Greek translation to highlight the fact that Jesus' words were quoted directly from Scripture (Psalm 22).

Subsequent episodes in John's Gospel, such as the division of Jesus' clothes by the soldiers (John 19:23-24), and the mention of Jesus' unbroken bones (John 19:32-37) underscore that Scripture had been fulfilled. Note that both of these were passive actions which someone hanging on a cross could not have had control over. But what is the point of emphasizing the fulfilment of Scripture over and over again?

Suffering that went beyond just fulfilling prophecies

When Jesus said, "I thirst," he was not complaining about being thirsty. These "fulfilled" words come from one of David's Psalms written centuries earlier, "I was thirsty, and they gave me vinegar to drink" (Psalm 69:21). David's life represents all kinds of human suffering: betrayal, abandonment, being misunderstood, despised, wrongly accused, and torment while suffering from thirst. Jesus' life on earth was to go through exactly what human suffering involved. While we know the significance of Jesus coming into the world was to die for the sins of the world, we also need to see his death as an extraordinary one. He chose a death that could best bear all the sufferings of mankind, to testify to the magnitude of God's love and His identification with humanity in our suffering, and His faithfulness to keep His promise of an everlasting covenant of love. And by doing so, God gives suffering an eternal meaning and purpose that is far beyond the suffering itself.

Choosing to die of his own accord

The final line Jesus said before his death is found in verse 30:

> When he had received the drink, Jesus said, "It is finished." With that, he bowed his head and gave up his spirit.

The last part of the verse literally means Jesus gave up his own soul. Some Bible translations say he surrendered his spirit to God. Though the original text in John only states he surrendered his spirit, it is not wrong to say Jesus gave up his spirit to the Father. Luke also records that Jesus called out, "Father, into your hands I commit my spirit" before breathing his last breath (Luke 23:46). In both gospels, the emphasis is on the fact that Jesus died of his own accord and surrendered his soul *voluntarily*. We probably rarely think of Jesus' death in this way. Very often we think in simplified terms, that since Jesus was nailed to the cross, he was killed. But the Biblical account showed that this was not the case. Jesus died of his own accord. He was not passively killed, but he had actively chosen the manner and timing of his death and gave up his spirit. This is something that man cannot do, but only God can do.

Remember in previous chapters we saw how John had made it clear that Jesus was not really betrayed (because he knew all of Judas' plot and even commanded Judas to go and carry out what he had planned to do). We also see that Jesus was not really captured (he chose to meet the captors, identify himself and follow them). Now we see that although Jesus was crucified, he was not passively killed, but had full control over his own death. All of this was to fulfil what Jesus had said of his life long ago, "No one takes it from me, but I lay it down of my own accord. I have authority to lay it down and authority to take it up again. This command I received from my Father" (John 10:18). It was a command from the Father, not from the governor.

When do we know that Jesus truly triumphed over death? Not only at the time of Jesus' resurrection later, but also at the moment he surrendered his soul. Jesus chose to enter death for us all by his own will and to overcome death for our sakes. He did it in order to save our souls so that we could also pass from death to life. Death is unavoidable for all of us and no one has power or authority over death, but Jesus is victorious over death and his authority is greater and more powerful than death. God overcame death for us.

A pierced body with no broken bones...

How do we know for sure? Verse 31 explains a tricky situation for the Jewish leaders at the time:

> Now it was the day of Preparation, and the next day was to be a special Sabbath. Because the Jewish leaders did not want the bodies left on the crosses during the Sabbath, they asked Pilate to have the legs broken and the bodies taken down.

Keeping the Sabbath holy was extremely important for the Jews, and it is stated clearly in their law that no dead body was to hang overnight during the Sabbath:

> **22** If someone guilty of a capital offense is put to death and their body is exposed on a pole, **23**you must not leave the body hanging on the pole overnight. Be sure to bury it that same day, because anyone who is hung on a pole is under God's curse. You must not desecrate the land the Lord your God is giving you as an inheritance. (Deuteronomy 21:22-23)

So, the idea that there were going to be three dead bodies hanging in public when the Sabbath was just about to start was absolutely unthinkable for the Jewish religious leaders. They were more concerned about the death of these three people on the crosses than the Roman executioners themselves, and they would do anything to accelerate their death so that they could remove and bury the bodies in time according to their customs. To ensure that this would happen, as a matter of urgency, they requested Pilate to have the men's legs broken, so that none of them could have the strength to raise their bodies to take any more breaths, and hence they would die within minutes.

After the Roman soldiers had broken the legs of the two men who had been crucified with Jesus, they came to Jesus and found that he was already dead, so they did not break his legs. Instead, to order to certify Jesus was truly dead, one of the soldiers pierced the side of Jesus' body with a spear, bringing a sudden flow of blood and water (John 19:32-34).

> **34** Instead, one of the soldiers pierced Jesus' side with a spear, bringing a sudden flow of blood and water. **35** The man who saw it has given testimony, and his testimony is true. He knows that he tells the truth, and he testifies so that you also may believe. **36** These things happened so that the scripture would be fulfilled: "Not one of his bones will be broken," **37** and, as another scripture says, "They will look on the one they have pierced."

So, again, John emphasizes two more details surrounding Jesus' death that had fulfilled prophecies in the Scriptures: that none of the Messiah's bones would be broken and that his body would be pierced. If they had had to break Jesus' legs to accelerate his death, then Jesus would have been killed rather than dying of his own accord. Not only that, Jesus died at the right time so that no one would break his legs and the soldiers would still have to pierce him with their spears as they needed to see both blood and water flowing out to officially verify his death.

What is the big deal about having not a single bone broken? Anyone who is familiar with the cultural context of the atonement lamb would understand perfectly. God gave clear detailed instructions for the Israelites when slaughtering the Passover Lamb, and one of the explicitly stated instructions was that they must not break any bone of the lamb (Exodus 12:46), which was not easy when slaughtering and dividing an animal for food. Jesus perfectly fulfilled every requirement of the Passover lamb that atones for our sins so that his perfect blood is sufficient to cover our sins. Jesus was the Passover Lamb God had prepared for our salvation. He died at three o'clock in the afternoon during Passover, the exact time when the Jews had to slaughter a lamb to prepare for the evening Passover meal.

The same applies to the piercing of his body. In Zechariah, it was prophesied that:

> "And I will pour out on the house of David and the inhabitants of Jerusalem a spirit of grace and supplication. They will look on me, the one they

have pierced, and they will mourn for him as one
mourns for an only child, and grieve bitterly for him
as one grieves for a firstborn son" (Zechariah 12:10)

In this prophecy from Zechariah, the piercing of the body signifies looking upon God and relying on Him for grace and supplication. This was exactly what God had prepared when His Son was hung on a cross. As we look upon the pierced body of Jesus, we are looking upon the grace of God the Father. And Jesus declared, "It is finished". We no longer have to look elsewhere for comfort, hope or answers. What is needed for your eternal reconciliation with God is all completed, all done, all accomplished, all fulfilled.

We have now seen the sheer number of Old Testament prophecies being fulfilled by a man being crucified on a cross within a short period of time. The odds of all these being fulfilled would have been absolutely impossible without the direct intervention of God Himself. He orchestrated every detail of that Passover weekend in order to indicate unmistakably that the man on the cross was indeed the Lamb God had promised for the world. Such is the magnitude of the determination, power, faithfulness and love of the Father.

As we look upon the pierced body of Jesus, we are looking at the Lamb who was the perfect atonement that our gracious Father had prepared for you and me.

It is finished.

DARKEST NIGHT, BRIGHTEST DAWN: A LENT REFLECTION

Reflection and Response

1. Which episode during Jesus' time on the cross has made the deepest impression on you? Why?
2. In what way is it important to you that prophecies regarding the Messiah were fulfilled in Jesus, both in his life and in his death?
3. How were God's justice and love reconciled in Jesus' death?
4. Jesus said, "It is finished." What exactly is finished? What difference does it make in your life?

Buried

.

(John 19:38-20:10)

.

19:38 Later, Joseph of Arimathea asked Pilate for the body of Jesus. Now Joseph was a disciple of Jesus, but secretly because he feared the Jewish leaders. With Pilate's permission, he came and took the body away. **39** He was accompanied by Nicodemus, the man who earlier had visited Jesus at night. Nicodemus brought a mixture of myrrh and aloes, about seventy-five pounds. **40** Taking Jesus' body, the two of them wrapped it, with the spices, in strips of linen. This was in accordance with Jewish burial customs. **41** At the place where Jesus was crucified, there was a garden, and in the garden a new tomb, in which no one had ever been laid. **42** Because it was the Jewish day of Preparation and since the tomb was nearby, they laid Jesus there.

20:1 Early on the first day of the week, while it was still dark, Mary Magdalene went to the tomb and saw that the stone had been removed from the entrance. **2** So she came running to Simon Peter and the other disciple, the one Jesus loved, and said, "They have taken the Lord out of the tomb, and we don't know where they have put him!"

3 So Peter and the other disciple started for the tomb. **4** Both were running, but the other disciple outran Peter and reached the tomb first. **5** He bent over and looked in at the strips of linen lying there but did not go in. **6** Then Simon Peter came along behind him and went straight into the tomb. He saw the strips of linen lying there, **7** as well as the cloth that had been wrapped around Jesus' head. The cloth was still lying in its place, separate from the linen. **8** Finally the other disciple, who had reached the tomb first, also went inside. He saw and believed. **9** (They still did not understand from Scripture that Jesus had to rise from the dead.) **10** Then the disciples went back to where they were staying.

Can you recall what you did between 3 and 6 PM last Friday afternoon?

Some of us may struggle to even recall what we did. Most of us who remember will probably answer "not much".

Three hours don't make up a long period of time at all. It passes so quickly. However, as we continue to reflect on Jesus' journey from crucifixion to his resurrection, I want to point out that on the very first Good Friday, many events of paramount importance happened to Jesus within those hours.

DARKEST NIGHT, BRIGHTEST DAWN: A LENT REFLECTION

What's so special about the time between 3 and 6 PM on Good Friday? Jesus died around 3 PM. At 6 PM, the Sabbath began. That weekend was not like any other Sabbath. It was the annual Passover festival. According to Jewish customs, people had to hurry home to get ready for the big weekend, as they were not meant to be doing any preparation once the Sabbath began around the time of sunset. Yet, as discussed before, the Jews had to have Jesus buried because leaving a dead body out in the open was a big taboo for the Sabbath and Passover according to the Law of Moses (Deuteronomy 21:22-23). In other words, within only three hours, the Jews must bring Jesus down from the cross (if they had permission from the Romans, of course), treat his body according to Jewish customs and complete his burial. That was quite an impossible task. One can imagine the hectic urgency and commotion people had to go through as they barely had time to deal with Jesus' dead body that afternoon, let alone reflect on what had just happened.

The events that unfolded during these three hours are also rarely discussed in our remembrance of Jesus' death in our Good Friday or Easter services at church. After reading about Jesus' last statement from the cross, "It is finished", we tend to think the story is finished and eagerly skip to the happy ending. However, Scripture provides us with a lot of detailed description of what happened during this time, and for this reason, I'd like to spend time reflecting on this often-neglected part of Jesus' journey.

The tricky task of proving a resurrection

To believe that Jesus' death and resurrection happened as an actual historical event is the core foundation of our Christian faith because the essence of the Gospel is that Jesus came to pay the price of death for our sins and triumphed over it. In order to claim that Jesus had genuinely risen from the dead, Christians must first prove that his death is historically verifiable. If we cannot prove that Jesus had died, then we can never make claims for his resurrection.

To prove resurrection as a historical event is a thorny, complex task. How exactly can you trace, investigate and prove beyond reasonable doubt that someone who was dead had risen back to life? Tracing what happened to Jesus' corpse is the key. There must be clearly documented information on where the body was laid, how it was treated, exactly how secure the location was and the eye-witness accounts testifying to what happened there afterwards, as well as their encounter with the live, resurrected person. All these details need to be specific and verifiable. Only then can we claim that the dead body had really disappeared and that there is no plausible explanation other than resurrection. The fact is, we do have such details.

God knew how important it was to provide us with historical proof of His Son's death and resurrection on earth. This is why the Bible devotes a part of the Gospel narrative to a series of events between Jesus' death on the cross and the beginning of the Sabbath. Did you notice that all four Gospels specifically identify three individuals by name when describing the events during this short period of time? Surprisingly, they were not Peter or John. In fact, none of them were from the group of the twelve disciples.

Pontius Pilate

The first of these individuals was Pontius Pilate. Why must all four Gospels mention him by name? Because he did not only sentence Jesus and approve his execution, he was also the one who officially certified Jesus' death on behalf of the Roman authorities. Scripture tells us that Pilate was actually surprised that Jesus died sooner than he thought he would (see previous chapter). One of the Roman soldiers pierced Jesus' side with a spear. When they saw both blood and water come out of his side, they were certain that Jesus had died. As far as the Roman court was concerned, Jesus was officially pronounced dead.

As discussed earlier, although the Jewish religious leaders thought they had finally managed to get rid of Jesus, now they could not allow dead bodies to be exposed in public when Passover began. This was a huge problem for them: who were they to ask the Roman governor to hand over the dead body of a high-profile defendant whom they had just accused of rebelling against the Empire? There was no way the Romans would sign the body off to them. Pilate would not care about Passover or Jewish customs. In addition, anyone who was viewed as an associate of Jesus would also be immediately implicated. This was why all of Jesus' disciples had scattered. No one would risk his life to file an application to obtain Jesus' body from the Romans on that day, especially when there were only three hours left before Passover began!

Joseph of where?

Then entered the second important man who was mentioned by all four Gospels: Joseph of Arimathea. Arimathea was a town quite far away from Jerusalem. We hardly know anything about this man, but he played a pivotal role in history because he was the one who buried Jesus. Between 3 PM and 6 PM that Friday, he was able to accomplish two near-impossible missions: to successfully obtain Jesus' body from the Romans while all the disciples had fled for their safety, and to immediately have at his disposal an elaborate, secured tomb. Whoever could achieve these was no simple man.

But why was Joseph willing to risk his life to ask Pilate to release Jesus' body to him? And how did he manage to convince Pilate to grant him permission? We know from Mark and Luke that he was a prominent member of the Council (Mark 15:43, Luke 23:50-51), a man of reputable status with a privileged position in society. This explains why he chose to be a follower of Jesus in secret: because of his fear of the religious leaders (John 19:38). The passage does make it sound as if Joseph was a coward, doesn't it? Either he was too scared to make his faith public, or he found it inconvenient to make it known that he was a disciple of Jesus. Yet God can use even a secret, fearful believer for His purpose and glory.

Mark and Luke also tell us he was a righteous man waiting for God's kingdom. Earlier, when others in the Council decided to prosecute Jesus, Joseph objected but was outnumbered. He could have kept silent both at the leaders' decision to arrest Jesus and later after Jesus' death, but he chose to do what he could for Jesus. While Jesus' closest friends had all run for their lives, the fact that Joseph came out to ask for Jesus' body from Pilate showed that he was no coward at all and was rewarded by receiving Pilate's favour. He took advantage of his social status and political influence to give Jesus a proper burial, something extremely important in Jewish culture in honouring the dead.

Joseph was placed in a unique position at that time in history, and he used it to accomplish what no one else could do for Jesus: to boldly go and meet Pilate (Mark 15:43) and ask for Jesus' body. God has gifted each of us a 'portion' (resources, circumstances, talents and gifts) for His purpose and glory. Is this how we view our own position and influence where God has placed us? Or do we only focus on how we can use these opportunities for ourselves? Do we have the courage to use what God has given us and take risks for God's sake? All your resources within your circumstance can be used by God at any time.

Now let's consider Jesus' tomb. What would have happened if Jesus hadn't had a tomb? If there had been no tomb, or if the Romans had simply discarded the body in any place, it would have been impossible to claim and verify there was ever a resurrection. But because of Joseph's action, we have a specific physical location where Jesus' body was lain which was known to both the Romans and the Jews.

Here's an alternative scenario which might have taken place: If Jesus' disciples had really believed Jesus' prediction that he would rise from the dead (John 12), then they would probably not have bothered with the burial. You wouldn't go through all the hassle of burying your loved one if you believed he or she would come back to life in three days, would you?

I would imagine Jesus' disciples would just sit back and watch over Jesus' body until he rose again. In this case, it would be impossible to make a convincing case later that Jesus had really risen from the dead as there would be no way for historians to trace the body. However, what happened was that the disciples were all on the run at the time, and so his burial had to be done by someone else.

Yet, who could have a new, empty tomb at his disposal at any time? Tombs were very important in Jewish culture as they showed the family's status and honour. Family members across different generations were usually buried together after they passed away, meaning their tombs were much bigger than our modern-day graves. Moreover, since Joseph was able to obtain Jesus' body from the Roman authorities as well as complete the burial within a short period of time, one can imagine the tomb he had for Jesus was in close proximity to Jerusalem. There was certainly no time to travel to a tomb that was far away if the burial must be completed by 6 PM. In other words, this new tomb was in a prime location.

In addition, we also know that this particular tomb was a pretty impressive one. Scripture points out that it was cut out from rock (Matthew 27:59-60, Mark 15:46, Luke 23:53), possibly one of the expensive kinds. Poorer families would only have a flimsy structure built with smaller stones as their family tombs. For Joseph's tomb, since it was carved out from rock, it would have been unmovable and with only one opening. Its prime location close to Jerusalem and its 'posh' style meant it was likely to cost a fortune and could have only been afforded by the wealthy.

DARKEST NIGHT, BRIGHTEST DAWN: A LENT REFLECTION

Another factor is that criminals on death row could not be buried with their family or others, so they either had no tomb or needed an unused tomb just for themselves. In other words, the value of Joseph's brand-new expensive tomb would have plummeted to zero the moment he placed Jesus' body inside. What a waste, especially when we know that it was only used for one weekend! Just like the woman who broke her alabaster jar for Jesus, Joseph gave up this precious tomb for his Lord. There was no turning back or holding back. Yet nothing goes to waste when given to God.

All these features, as detailed by Scripture, are the essential basis of tangible evidence for anyone who wants to investigate the historical reliability of Jesus' resurrection.

Although Joseph had not professed his faith in Jesus openly in public previously, his boldness in taking risks for Jesus and his readiness in sacrificing his prized resources, revealed his love for Jesus. Indeed, it was God who prepared the tomb and provided Joseph with the resources. But Joseph could have easily sat back quietly and taken no action, especially under such hectic circumstances and the tense political atmosphere of the time. He probably had no time to sit down and calculate his cost, but he was willing and ready to surrender what he had when he saw the opportunity right in front of him. What about us? How would we have reacted if we had been in Joseph's shoes?

Nicodemus

The third person that appeared in all four Gospels was, of course, Mary, the first witness of Jesus' resurrection. But we'll reflect on her story in the next chapter. Before jumping to Easter Sunday, let's also reflect on another interesting individual that appeared within the critical three hours between Jesus' death and resurrection—Nicodemus, the same man who asked Jesus about the meaning of being born again (John 3). Now he suddenly reappears in John 19:39-42:

> **39** He was accompanied by Nicodemus, the man who earlier had visited Jesus at night. Nicodemus brought a mixture of myrrh and aloes, about seventy-five pounds. **40** Taking Jesus' body, the two of them wrapped it, with the spices, in strips of linen. This was in accordance with Jewish burial customs.
>
> **41** At the place where Jesus was crucified, there was a garden, and in the garden a new tomb, in which no one had ever been laid. **42** Because it was the Jewish day of Preparation and since the tomb was nearby, they laid Jesus there.

Like Joseph of Arimathea, Nicodemus was also a man of reputable social status as well as a 'hidden' follower of Jesus. The last time we read about him was in John 3, when he went to meet Jesus at night. His status could have also meant it was not too convenient for him to be an open disciple and, again like

DARKEST NIGHT, BRIGHTEST DAWN: A LENT REFLECTION

Joseph, these three hours after Jesus' death was an opportune time for him to come out and help out in Jesus' most helpless moment.

Nicodemus' crucial role in Jesus' burial was providing the myrrh and aloes needed to anoint Jesus' body (and he bought a lot with him—75 pounds, or 34 kilograms!) and strips of linen to wrap around it. Throughout Jesus' life on earth, there were two times when he was totally helpless: when he was born and when he was dead on the cross. In both situations, someone offered myrrh, a very valuable, costly gift to offer. Yet have you ever wondered what good myrrh could do for a newborn baby and someone who's dead? Nothing of practical use at all. But it is a sign of worship, of honouring the worthiness of Jesus, of acknowledging his royalty and kingship.

Unlike the expensive myrrh, there was nothing glamorous about the strips of linen Nicodemus brought to Jesus; they were, after all, only used for wrapping dead bodies. However, later this linen was to become the very first piece of physical evidence in history for Jesus' resurrection. Without the linen, if there had been only an empty tomb, there might still have been different ways of explaining the disappearance of the body, such as someone stealing it in the middle of the night or some animals sneaking into the tomb and devouring it. But the linen that Nicodemus had used turned out to be proof that is hard to dispute because of its peculiar condition when it was discovered that Sunday morning:

> **3** So Peter and the other disciple started for the tomb. **4** Both were running, but the other disciple outran Peter and reached the tomb first. **5** He bent

over and looked in at the strips of linen lying there but did not go in. **6** Then Simon Peter came along behind him and went straight into the tomb. He saw the strips of linen lying there, **7** as well as the cloth that had been wrapped around Jesus' head. The cloth was still lying in its place, separate from the linen.

8 Finally the other disciple, who had reached the tomb first, also went inside. He saw and believed. **9** (They still did not understand from Scripture that Jesus had to rise from the dead.) **10**Then the disciples went back to where they were staying.

When the disciples realised that the body was gone, the first thing they feared was that someone had stolen the body. It was only when John and Peter looked into the tomb and saw the strips of linen lying there that they knew this was not a case of theft. Anyone who had wanted to steal a dead body from a tomb of a high-profile figure guarded by Roman soldiers would not have had the time or intention to unwrap the linen mixed with a large quantity of myrrh and aloes as it would have been incredibly messy, time-consuming and totally unnecessary. Notice the passage still emphasizes that they did not understand that Jesus had indeed risen from the dead. So why did the linen make them believe? They saw that the cloth that had been wrapped around Jesus' head was still lying in its place, separate from the linen (Verses 7-8).

Have you ever wondered exactly how Jesus rose from the dead while his body was wrapped in linen and a large amount of myrrh? Remember in Lazarus' story, Jesus had to command people to free him from the cloth and linen (John 11:44) as it was Jewish custom to wrap the body in many layers of cloth with ointments in between before placing it in the tomb. After a while, the linen and the skin of the body would be stuck together, so it was rather difficult for Lazarus to free himself after Jesus raised him from the dead.

In Jesus' case, however, the cloth for the head was still lying in its place and separate from the rest of the linen, so by looking at the inside of the rolls of cloth and linen, John and Peter could see that the body had simply vanished. If the body had been stolen, the wrapping materials would have also been taken, together with the large amount of myrrh and aloes glued to the body by then. Even if the thief had really tried to remove the linen strips before taking the body, the strips would have to be torn off in a chaotic manner and strewn all over the place. Perhaps Nicodemus didn't think much of what he had done for Jesus, but it turned out to provide a crucial piece of evidence for Jesus' resurrection.

A short-lived burial with eternal significance

On that Good Friday, while all of Jesus' closest friends had vanished from the scene, two men of considerable social stature and resources suddenly appeared from nowhere and did what they could with what they had at their disposal to accomplish three impossible tasks in three hours: 1) request and retrieve

Jesus' body from the Roman court; 2) anoint and treat the body properly; and 3) give Jesus a proper burial in a secured tomb at just the right time. The fact that these were all done in three hours suggests that there was probably a team of capable helpers commanded by Joseph and Nicodemus involved as well. There must have been a lot of deploying, organizing, logistics and transport, as well as emotions of course.

Between these two secret followers of Jesus, a large chunk of their wealth vanished in a moment as they rushed to pay their final respects to the Messiah they believed in, not expecting to have anything in return. They probably thought that they were only honouring the dead according to their usual customs, and these acts were the last thing they could do for Jesus after witnessing his gruesome death. Little did they know that God would use their resources and actions to build a solid case for the most important event in human history. Many pieces of the circumstantial evidence we have today for the resurrection are related to the rare specifications of this particular tomb and the way the linen was later found. Without either of these, we can make up all sorts of alternative theories about what happened to Jesus' body. But with both Joseph's tomb and Nicodemus' myrrh and linen, there is only one explanation that fits all the circumstantial evidence.

Tombs and strips of linen are not glamorous things that we would associate with the Kingdom of God. Many of us may often wonder whether we have anything great or worthy to give to God. But who is the true master of our wealth and resources?

DARKEST NIGHT, BRIGHTEST DAWN: A LENT REFLECTION

When we surrender our God-given resources back to God, we never know how He will use them to accomplish impossible goals beyond our understanding. When we are doing ordinary tasks that God has called us to do, we don't often see the extraordinary eternal purpose. Yet what we can learn from Joseph and Nicodemus was their tremendous generosity in sacrificing their resources, their swift readiness to take action, and boldness in taking risks to come out in the open as they did what they believed was right to do for Jesus. They were ready to act when Jesus needed them to, and what they provided for Jesus that Good Friday set the scene for the coming Sunday morning.

Reflection and Response

1. What would be going through your mind if you had helped in the burial of Jesus?
2. How do we view our resources and possessions on earth today? How is your attitude demonstrated in the way you manage them?
3. Jesus surrendered all on the cross for us. How ready are we to surrender all of what we have and risk it all for Jesus? Have you ever come across such an opportunity?

Risen

.

(John 20: 1-18)

.

Our Lent journey started with the story of Judas on the night of the betrayal, which helped us to contemplate the reality of sin. Jesus' example of praying in Gethsemane led us to ponder how we face our own weaknesses. Later, his arrest and the disciples' troubled reactions helped us to reflect on our brokenness in times of crisis, while the highly unusual trial of Jesus conducted by Pilate helped us to see how God's ultimate sovereignty and His covenant of love were woven together in history. We also looked at Jesus during the time he was on the cross as we meditated on death and our relationship with God. Finally, we saw a story of sacrifice and worship as we read about how two men used their resources and positions to do what they could for Jesus' burial at a timely and opportune moment. Now we're finally coming to the resurrection.

Mary was the first person to encounter the risen Jesus, so technically that qualifies her as the first person ever to enter a new era in human history. Yet she entered this joyful era with utter sadness. Let's read the story found in John 20: 1-18. While you're reading, can you identify one particular verb that is used by the author a total of seven times?

> **1** Early on the first day of the week, while it was still dark, Mary Magdalene went to the tomb and saw that the stone had been removed from the entrance. **2** So she came running to Simon Peter and the other disciple, the one Jesus loved, and said, "They have taken the Lord out of the tomb, and we don't know where they have put him!"

> **3** So Peter and the other disciple started for the tomb. **4** Both were running, but the other disciple outran Peter and reached the tomb first. **5** He bent over and looked in at the strips of linen lying there but did not go in. **6** Then Simon Peter came along behind him and went straight into the tomb. He saw the strips of linen lying there, **7** as well as the cloth that had been wrapped around Jesus' head. The cloth was still lying in its place, separate from the linen. **8** Finally the other disciple, who had reached the tomb first, also went inside. He saw and believed. **9** (They still did not understand from Scripture that Jesus had to rise from the dead.) **10** Then the disciples went back to where they were staying.

11 Now Mary stood outside the tomb crying. As she wept, she bent over to look into the tomb **12** and saw two angels in white, seated where Jesus' body had been, one at the head and the other at the foot.

13 They asked her, "Woman, why are you crying?"

"They have taken my Lord away," she said, "and I don't know where they have put him." **14** At this, she turned around and saw Jesus standing there, but she did not realize that it was Jesus.

15 He asked her, "Woman, why are you crying? Who is it you are looking for?"

Thinking he was the gardener, she said, "Sir, if you have carried him away, tell me where you have put him, and I will get him."

16 Jesus said to her, "Mary."

She turned toward him and cried out in Aramaic, "Rabboni!" (which means "Teacher").

17 Jesus said, "Do not hold on to me, for I have not yet ascended to the Father. Go instead to my brothers and tell them, 'I am ascending to my Father and your Father, to my God and your God.'"

18 Mary Magdalene went to the disciples with the news: "I have seen the Lord!" And she told them that he had said these things to her.

Can you 'see'?

The verb 'to see' is repeated seven times here. Encountering the risen Jesus requires us to 'see' again and again before we can finally see him. Mary could see many things at first, but she couldn't really see. She saw the stone had been moved, and immediately she thought of the worst-case scenario: Jesus' body must have been taken by someone. That was not a very logical conclusion as tomb raiders of her time usually stole treasures, not corpses. After knowing Jesus so intimately and even witnessing him raising the dead, Mary didn't seem to remember anything Jesus had said about himself. She was so agitated she had only one thing on her mind: Jesus' dead body. Not seeing the body threw her into despair and panic. As far as she was concerned, Jesus' corpse was the only thing in the world she desperately wanted to find.

John and Peter quickly arrived at the tomb and tried to see a bit more closely. They examined the inside of the tomb and saw the linen and cloth that were once used on Jesus' body (verses 6-7). The way the linen and cloth were laid suggested to them that the body was not stolen, but they had to hurry back home, probably still trying to process what had just happened. As Jesus' crucifixion was a very high-profile case, his disciples were still in danger of being seen in public as they could be arrested as well. They took the risk coming to check on the tomb and quickly headed back home to avoid being seen.

Mary stayed, overwhelmed with sorrow. Next, she saw two angels. Imagine seeing two angels! For many of us, seeing two angels would be enough to wake us up and snap us out of our thoughts into reality. Yet Mary still couldn't 'see'. She was too taken up with her own grief and despair, trapped in her false understanding and assumption about what had happened.

The angels had to ask her, "Why are you crying?", a seemingly insensitive question to ask a woman mourning the death of a loved one at a tomb. Sometimes God has to ask the most obvious questions to wake us up: What are we so sad about? Why are we crying?

Seeing an empty tomb didn't help Mary. Apparently seeing two angels didn't help either. Now, would seeing Jesus standing right in front of her make a difference? In verse 14, she even saw Jesus with her own eyes! But her emotions were so overwhelming for her that she had no idea what she was seeing. Her grief, sorrow, hopelessness and anxiety had meant she was fixated on her self-created version of reality. Her desperation to find the dead Jesus blinded her from seeing the risen Jesus. Little did she realise that what she was futilely seeking was not what she really needed. She needed to see the risen Jesus.

Just like Mary's misery that Easter morning, very often our fraught mind creates an alternative reality based on our wrong assumptions. We are blinded from seeing God's power and deliverance as our minds are preoccupied with the wrong questions, wrong focus, wrong goals. Like Mary, we can 'see' Jesus, but can't really *see* Jesus. There are simply too many obstacles in our hearts and minds, including emotional, cognitive, and spiritual ones. Have you been in this situation?

To be fair, we can't blame Mary for not recognising Jesus. Later, we find out pretty much everyone else who knew Jesus very well also couldn't recognise him initially either. The notion of a risen Jesus was not easy to comprehend fully in a short period of time after the traumatic event only a few days before. Seeing her loved one's body being battered and cruelly nailed to a cross, Mary was not in a place of thinking hopeful thoughts. Everyone needs the risen Jesus to help them see and recognise him. So how did Jesus help Mary see in the end?

"Who is it you are looking for?"

Jesus had to ask her the same question,

> "Woman, why are you crying? Who is it you are looking for?" (verse 15).

Notice Jesus' second question started with "who", not "what". Why is this significant? We are to look for a living person, not a dead one. Mary was still pleading for a corpse,

> "Sir, if you have carried him away, tell me where you have put him, and I will get him."

She still believed she had to go and find Jesus and do something for him. But Jesus had already said, "It is finished." He has done everything for us. We don't find Jesus. Jesus finds us.

Then Jesus did something very simple to help Mary see. He simply said one word, her name:

> Jesus said to her, "Mary." Mary turned toward him and cried out in Aramaic, "Rabboni!" (which means "Teacher") (verse 16).

What an instantaneous transformation! Let's look at it closely. Isn't it strange that Jesus only called her name and, all of a sudden, she realized the gardener she thought she had been talking to was Jesus himself?

What's in a name?

To fully appreciate the significance of a spoken word, we need to look at the response from its recipient. Here the author deliberately chose to quote the original expression used by Mary rather than translating it into Greek. Aramaic was the spoken dialect of the time; the dialect Mary and Jesus would have often used with each other. Although we can't tell from the text, the tone or accent in which Jesus called Mary's name must have been such a unique, familiar sound to Mary that it allowed her to instantly realise that the person in front of her must unmistakably be Jesus himself. As in any intimate human relationship, the way a loved one's name is called often carries a certain familiar uniqueness that is instinctively recognised by the one being called. This is a sign of intimacy, connection and knowledge of each other.

What Mary really needed was not logical explanations or miracles and signs, but to simply hear Jesus call her by her name. The familiarity immediately woke her up and opened her eyes. Hearing Jesus calling her name reminded her of the close friendship they once shared and brought her out of her misery and into joy and reconnection with her Lord.

An encounter with the risen Jesus is an experience that brings an indescribable peace and satisfaction. Those who have tasted it can immediately recognise it. No one can explain it in words. Often, the living Jesus is standing right in front of us when we are mindlessly searching for something dead and hopeless. What we need is to hear Jesus' voice calling us by name and reconnecting us with the reality of the risen Jesus being with us.

Some religions boast about having grand lavish tombs for their deceased religious leaders, with expensive artefacts and the real corpses still inside. We Christians, however, like to boast about a dull, empty tomb. It's empty, for "he is not here, he has risen!" The very fact that it's empty is the unique trademark and cornerstone of our faith which no other faith system in this world could ever boast about. Only one person in history has conquered death. Only one person has the power to promise us genuine peace, hope for eternity and reconciliation with God.

Do NOT hold onto Jesus?

What Jesus said to Mary next was somewhat perplexing,

> "Do not hold on to me, for I have not yet ascended to the Father. Go instead to my brothers and tell them, 'I am ascending to my Father and your Father, to my God and your God.'"

Do not hold on to Jesus? Isn't that what all Christians are meant to do? Of course, after recognising Jesus, the only thing Mary wanted to do was to hold onto Jesus forever. Shouldn't they go and reunite with everyone else and celebrate together, and then everyone could live happily ever after? What a surprising command coming from Jesus. Wouldn't it be great if Jesus could stay longer to plant a few churches, start some leadership training courses for the disciples (they were literally fleeing or denying Jesus just a couple of days ago!), teach and perform more miracles?

Yet Jesus told Mary not to hold onto him. Not only that, Jesus even told her to go and tell the other disciples that he was ascending to his Father. That was a very serious announcement. Why didn't Jesus go to them himself and tell them this important message directly? Note in the Jewish customs of the time, women's testimonies did not carry any weight at all in court. So it was bizarre for Jesus to ask a woman to bear witness for him when he himself could have done it.

A whole new life

Encountering the risen Jesus meant the start of a whole new relationship, a whole new experience and a whole new world. No one remains the same after meeting the risen Jesus. Mary and the disciples' lives were so thoroughly transformed that they were sent into the world as representatives of Jesus himself. Mary had seen the risen Jesus and she was now ready to witness for Jesus and speak to the world on behalf of Jesus. She was now his representative. Jesus' resurrection empowered all who believed in him with unlimited possibilities to serve him. Indeed, the very first historical account of Jesus' resurrection we have today is from Mary herself: "I have seen the Lord!"

Reflection and Response

1. Mary's initial sorrow and desperation compelled her to seek a dead Jesus and blinded her from seeing the risen Jesus. In what ways could we be like Mary?
2. In your encounter with the risen Jesus, what did Jesus do to open your eyes to see him?
3. How important is the empty tomb to your faith?
4. After recognising the resurrected Jesus, his disciples experienced a total transformation in their faith, boldness and relationship with him. Is such life-changing transformation visible in your walk with Jesus?

Also by Dr. Philip Yeung

Jesus' Awkward Questions
ISBN: 9798201322373 (Paperback)
9798201353797 (eBook)

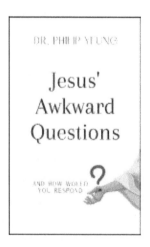

Jesus asked many questions during his three years of ministry on earth, some provocative, some unsettling, and some rather strange! In *Jesus' Awkward Questions*, a medical doctor and Biblical Greek scholar dissects 12 stories where Jesus asked a peculiar question, and reflects on what Jesus was revealing about himself and the human condition, and how radically he speaks to our lives today.

PHILIP YEUNG

Publications in Chinese

.

楊醫職場靈思：從創造到召命的信仰對話
A Dialogue of Spiritual Engagements at the
Marketplace: from Creation to Calling
Publisher: Inpress
ISBN: 9789624576207 (Paperback)

平凡人生，超凡召命：楊錫鏘牧師講道集
Heavenly Calling in a Down-to-Earth Life:
Dr Philip Yeung's Sermon Collection
ISBN: 9781792376054 (Paperback)

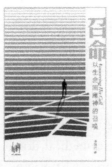

召命：以生命回應神的召喚
Answering His Call
Publisher: Christian Communications
ISBN: 9789887768265 (Paperback)

DARKEST NIGHT, BRIGHTEST DAWN: A LENT REFLECTION

回歸聖言之導引
A Call to Follow the Way
Publisher: Christian Communications
ISBN: 9789881612045 (Paperback)

回歸聖言之陶造
The Word: a Call to Transformation
Publisher: Christian Communications
ISBN: 9789881611895 (Paperback)

回歸聖言之召喚
The WORD: A Homecoming Call
Publisher: Christian Communications
ISBN: 9789881611871 (Paperback)

About the Author

Rev. Dr. Philip Yeung (Yeung Sek Cheung) was raised in Hong Kong and trained as a medical doctor at the University of Hong Kong. Five years into his practice, he believed God called him to leave his profession to serve in theological education in Hong Kong. After graduating from Regent College, Canada, he devoted the next 40 years of his life to teaching at China Graduate School of Theology, where he specialized in the teaching of biblical languages, the books of Genesis, Job and Ecclesiastes, as well as homiletics and pastoral care. His medical training, his proficiency in both Biblical Hebrew and Greek, and his journey in discovering God's calling, all equipped him with insights into stories in the Bible as well as the ability to dissect them and help his students apply them in modern life.

Lightning Source UK Ltd.
Milton Keynes UK
UKHW011316100223
416824UK00022B/837